MW00613416

Gypsy Magic

for the Lover's Soul

Gypsy Magic

for the Lover's Soul

A Romany Book of Spells, Sachets, Oils and Incense

Allie Theiss

GYPSYGIRL
PRESS

NOTE: The intent of the author is only to offer practices, techniques and formulas to help you in your quest for emotional, mental, spiritual and physical empowerment. They should not be used as an alternative to professional medical, legal, mental, financial treatment and/or advice. Nor should it be used as an alternative to common sense. In the event you use any of the information in the book for yourself, which is your Divinely inspired right, the author and the publisher assume no responsibility for your actions.

ISBN-13 978-0-9771835-0-0
ISBN-10 0-9771835-0-5
LCCN: 2006923398

Cover design by L. Hughes
Editing by K.M.
Interior illustrations by J. Rowlett
Interior design by L. Hughes

Gypsy Girl Press does not participate in, endorse, or have any authority or responsibility concerning private business transactions between our authors and the public. All mail addressed to the author is forwarded but the publisher cannot, unless specifically instructed by the author, give out the author's address of phone number.

Gypsy Girl Press
P.O. Box 1511
Wooster, OH 44691
authorfeedback@gypsygirlpress.net
http://www.GypsyGirlPress.net

ATTENTION CORPORATIONS, UNIVERSITIES, COLLEGES, AND PROFESSIONAL ORGANIZATIONS: Quality discounts are available on bulk purchases of this book for educational, gift purposes, or as premiums for increasing magazine subscriptions or renewals. Special books or book excerpts can also be created to fit specific needs. For information, contact Gypsy Girl Press, P.O. Box 1511, Wooster, OH 44691; ph 330.264.9977

To God, the Goddess Brigit, my guides: Robert and Hanna, my archangels: Michael, Raphael, Gabriel, Haniel, Jeremiel and Jesus -- my eternal gratitude, love and appreciation for their Divine wisdom, love and guidance.

Table of Contents

Gypsy Lore

History of the Roma

Diverse, nomadic…to be Roma, or "gypsy," is to be a member of an ethnic minority that is difficult to define. Throughout their history, the Roma have been comprised of many different groups of people, absorbing outsiders and other cultures while migrating across continents. This has resulted in creating a patchwork of groups calling themselves Roma, each with differing cultures, customs, and written languages.

Despite their differences, the Roma do share certain attributes. Made up of four "tribes," or nations (*natsiya*), they are bound together at least through Rom blood and Romani (or Romanes), the root language they share. The Roma also hold common characteristics: they are extremely loyal to family and clan; a strong belief in both *Del* (God) and *Beng* (the Devil); belief in predestiny; and Romaniya, loosely translated as certain standards and norms in codes of conduct (which vary in degree from tribe to tribe). At their core, because of their history, they are a people who are adaptable to changing conditions.

No one knows where the Roma originated. Because they arrived in Europe from the East, they were thought by early Europeans to be from Turkey or Nubia or any one of vaguely acknowledged non-European places. They were even thought to have been from Egypt, and were called, among other things, Egyptians, or 'Gyptians, which is how the word "Gypsy" originated.

In the second half of the 18th century, European scholars studying the Roma found that the Romani language shared basic words, including numbers, action, family relationships, etc. with the Eastern Indian languages. Indeed, its roots appear to be based on Sanskrit, the historical language of the Hindus of India.

While Romani has many dialects, it is a spoken-only language. There are, still, many common words used by each dialect. Thus, based on language alone the Roma are divided into three subgroups: the *Domari* of the Middle East and Eastern Europe (the *Dom*), the Lomarvren of Central Europe (the *Lom*), and the Romani of Western Europe (the *Rom*). Among themselves the Roma speak their own language; otherwise they speak the language of the country they currently occupy.

Today there are approximately more than twelve million Roma living across the world. It's difficult to put a final tally on their numbers, as many Roma lie about their heritage due to economic, social and political reasons.

Great migrations through Roma history has dispersed them throughout the world, beginning with the first wave when it is assumed they left India over a thousand years ago. The next great move, known as the *Aresajipe*, was from southwest Asia into Europe during the 14th century. The third great migration was from Europe to the United States during the 19th century and early 20th century after the abolishment of Romani slavery in Europe.

The wheel above represents a sixteen-spoked chakra, which is the Romani symbol. A chakra is a link back to the Roma's Indian ancestry (India has the 24-spoked Ashok Chakra in the center of their flag) and represents movement forward and Creation. The Romani flag is green and blue with a red chakra in the center. The Roma motto is "*Opré Roma*" (Roma Arise) and the song "*Gelem, gelem*," also known as "*Djelem, djelem*" and "*Opré Roma*," is the Romani anthem.

Although the Romas have been subjected to centuries of abuse, the most notable being the *Porrajmos* (Holocaust) during World War II, responsible for millions of senseless deaths, Romany communities can be found all over the world including the United States. No longer do they wander the earth in a horse-drawn caravan, but are modernized and travel by car, bus and plane.

The very definition of "free spirits," the Roma have lived a nomadic existence for as long as they have been on earth and have lived in harmony with nature longer than most. With a kinship to mind, body and soul that we can only dream of, the Roma have much to teach.

Check out the other books in this series for more Gypsy Lore that will cover: families, the holocaust, fortune telling and Shamanism.

What is Magic?

The easiest way to tell you what magic is, is to tell you what it isn't: a quick fix. Instant gratification only arrives in the movies or on TV. There is no real *Harry Potter* or *Charmed* magic – at least nothing we mere mortals can conjure up.

At its simplest, magic is the ability to manipulate energy, to direct it to where we need a little extra guidance. When a spell is cast, we are giving our energy an added push to help us achieve a dream or goal. Magic is an added boost – a leg up if you will – but be forewarned that it can take up to six months to a year in order to see the

fruits of your labor. Sometimes, however, if you're lucky you can start to see results in as little as twenty-four hours.

The energy that surges within each of our bodies is the same energy that soars through the universe and on up into the heavens. It is all around us twenty-four hours a day, seven days a week. Therefore, it is within your reach to take the energy you need to bring about the changes you desire – no special gifts or powers required. Each and every one of us is already blessed with the Divine gifts we require. But to have your magic work, you must firmly and sincerely believe, without a doubt, that you will achieve the results you need. Anything less will result in either complete failure or level of success only achieved by half.

The material in this book is a wonderful way for you to effectively send off your will and determination into the Universe to create the changes you require. There are different ingredients and props used in each quest, and are an important part of connecting you to the energy of the Divine. However, the most important ingredient for a successful outcome is thought.

Or, look at it another way: Our thoughts are comprised of energy, energy that we normally allow to jump from place to place, person to person throughout the day. Thus, your thoughts affect the people around you as well as impact your life in ways large and small. Since most of the time we do not put forth the effort to control our thoughts, our lives always seem to be awash in confusion.

Magic helps you concentrate your thoughts towards a specific outcome or goal. Once your focus is centered, clear and full of positive passion, determination and resolve, you raise your vibrational rate to match the energy of the Divine. Once your awareness is raised, you can manifest whatever it is that you desire, receiving what your thoughts project. This gives a whole new layer to the phrase, "Be careful what you wish for, as you just might get it."

By tapping into the Divine, where all of our unconscious minds are eternally linked, you are able to influence a person's thought process on an unconscious level, thereby affecting their life on a conscious level. So, magic is nothing more – and nothing less – than having the ability to manipulate the energy around you. We all have the power to make change.

Just think what you can accomplish if you set your mind to it!

Preparing Yourself and Your Space for Magic.

It is never a good idea just to jump in and start doing magic. It is important to prepare the space and the personal energy that will support your cause.

Prepare Yourself

• Take a bath or shower. Disposing of the physical filth picked up during the day and washing it away will help you perform better and develop better concentration. When you feel clean, the energy around you does, as well.

• Refrain from drinking caffeine or alcohol at least an hour prior to the magic.

• Make sure that you are not hungry or thirsty, as feeling either can take your focus away from the task at hand.

• Wear comfortable clothes.

• Meditate for at least 10 minutes before you begin performing magic. This helps to calm your mind and push out the clutter of daily thoughts that could interfere with the energy process.

Prepare Your Space

• Make sure the room is clean. Dust and vacuum the day of or the day before.

• Throw or put away any junk (mail, dirty clothes, dirty dishes, etc…) that is lying around.

• Weather permitting, open a window to allow the fresh air and added energy into your room.

• Burn Frankincense or Bay leaves, being careful to disperse the smoke around the room. As you do so, visualize any and all negativity leaving your space.

• Turn on soft lighting to create the right atmosphere.

A little bit of preparation goes a long way! Observe the difference by preparing and not preparing before magic…and note the results.

Tips for Successful Magic

• Turn off the phone, radio, email, or anything else that will disturb you during the process. However, soothing music may be played as you prepare and perform magic. The key here is that you want no interruptions.

• Keep the tools you use for magic away from other people, as tools absorb the energy of their user.

• Consult a calendar to time your magic with the ebb and flow of the lunar cycle.

• Magic has a very hard time working correctly during a Mercury Retrograde and should be avoided during this time. Mercury goes backwards (retrograde) four times a year and usually lasts about three weeks. Since Mercury is the planet of communications, you want it to be moving direct for positive results.

• What you send out comes back to you three times over, so if you are using magic to hurt or make someone else feel uncomfortable, you do so at your own risk.

• Keep your magic to yourself. When you tell others of your plans, you invite their energy to mingle in with yours. This can weaken your energy, thereby weakening the energy of your magic.

• Think positively about the changes you desire, but don't dwell on them. By detaching yourself you let the uni-verse help as well. Detaching doesn't decrease the power of your want, but it does give the universe permission to step in and take over.

• Remember that impa-tience leads to doubt and doubt invites negativity. Neither nature nor the uni-verse can be rushed. Magic works in Divine time, not human time.

• Remember above all that faith in yourself, faith in magic and positive thoughts are all powerful vibratory forces that bring results.

Tips for your Adopted Stone Spirits

Adopting Stone Spirits

When adopting stone spirits, adopt only from caretakers who have been kind to the spirits while in their care. This includes those involved in the harvesting of the stone spirits. When stone spirits are used out of greed and not love, you will feel the negative vibrations from the stone.

The more we adopt spirits from those greedy people, the longer Mother Earth will be mutilated for greed. To find a supplier who does support the spirits in love, ask for referrals from friends, family or those who are involved with stones on a professional level.

It is just as easy to pick a stone spirit online as it is in person. You will know which one is for you; there will be a stirring inside you as the stone tries to communicate its desire to come home with you.

Imperfect spirits or raw stones can be just as helpful and loving as their beautiful counterparts. You can't judge a rock by its cover!

Cleaning Stones

Stones are subjected to a multitude of energies before they arrive in your home. Prior to using them in magic, it is advised that you perform a cleansing or purification ritual on the stones. However, it is always preferable to listen to your stones/crystals first to "hear" if they require a cleansing. I personally have 1000+ stones and I think I have cleansed only a few hundred. This is a very simple process, one which removes any and all past influences from the stone making it ready for your use. There are a number of different methods of cleansing a stone:

1 Place the stone in full sunlight for one day, 3 days, or even a week. It's best to place it in direct sunlight, and not behind a window on a ledge. Some stones will clear after a day, while others will take longer. Check the stone daily and sense its energies by placing it in your receptive hand (left hand if you are right handed, opposite if you are left handed). If the vibrations are regular, the cleansing has been successful.

IMPORTANT: Some stones will damage/fade in the sun. Be sure to check your stone frequently.

2 Bury the stone in the ground for a week or so, then check to see if it has been purified. If it has, wash it off and begin your magic.

3 Run the stone under running water and wipe off with a white cloth. Check to see if it has been purified. If not, then simply repeat the process.

4 Another popular method is to use sea salt. You can either mix the salt with water and then soak the stone or rub the salt directly onto the stone.

IMPORTANT: Some stones can become damaged by the salt's harshness. If you are not sure whether your stone will be adversely affected by the salt then avoid it altogether. Rule of thumb: The softer the stone the harsher the damage.

5 Place the stone outside (if you can) at the start of a full moon for three nights.

6 Burn sage and pass the stone through the smoke. I have found this to be the most effective method but again, do what you feel is right for yourself and your stone.

Charging Stones

Many sources state that before using stones in magic, they should be "charged" or "programmed" with energy for the specific purpose you plan on using the stone. My own thought on this is that "programming" is simply wrong. I feel as though you are forcing your own will on the stone, forcing it to do something against its will. Think of it as trying to potty train a cat. Eventually, the cat can be trained, but your relationship with the cat will suffer in the process.

On the other hand, "charging" is a completely different matter. Charging encourages or awakens the stone to help you or someone else, using the properties it already possesses. By charging the stone, you are merely asking for help.

"Charging" is simply done by holding the stones in your projective hand (right if right handed - left if left handed), visualizing your magical need, and pouring energy out from your body into the stone.

For example, if you have a Moonstone and need to get more sleep at night, put the Moonstone into your projective hand and visualize yourself sleeping, pouring your energy from you into the stone. Once you can feel the vibrations, you'll know that the stone has been charged.

You may also want to ask the stone if it simply needs a "boost." Many do not need the encouragement to help - they share their knowledge and powers willingly. In the Spells chapter it is encouraged that you to add the extra energy to the stone spirits for maximum benefit.

FREE GIFT

Do you believe in love at first sight?

Want to find your soul mate -- without spending a fortune?

I am asked by clients all over the world, "When will I meet my soul mate?" Through mostly trial and error over the last 20 years, I've discovered who my soul mate is and how to psychically connect. And now, I want to pass that knowledge on to you.

Visit now and receive absolutely **FREE** a booklet based on my popular workshop: **"Soul Mate Quest."**

To learn what intuitive people know that most people don't, register for the **FREE** booklet by going to **http://www.gypsyadvice.com/smq.htm**. What you'll discover in the booklet will be valuable information and techniques that you can turn to time and time again, information such as:

Definition of a soul mate • Simple connection techniques Astral sex • ...and so much more!

To register for the FREE booklet, go here now:

http://www.gypsyadvice.com/smq.htm

I look forward to helping you find whom you've been missing!

Crystal Sunshine!
Allie :)

Incenses

Incense has smoldered around gypsy camps for centuries, lit to attract specific energies, aid in attracting a certain goal, or ward off people, places and things from personal space. Incense emits specific vibrations to facilitate transformation. Its energies mix with those of the seeker to speed up the changes needed to reach a desired goal.

Supplies

Mortar and pestle or electric grinder
Non-metal bowl
Glass jar with lid
Charcoal block
Censer

Making Incense

1. If not purchased pre-powdered, grind each herb into a fine powder using either mortar and pestle or an electric grinder.
2. Add each herb into your bowl.
3. Visualize your need or goal.
4. Once it has been clearly formed in your mind, using your projective hand (right if right-handed, left if left-handed) mix the herbs as the images from your mind transfer down your arm, through your hand and empower the herbs.
5. Store in a tightly capped jar or burn on a block of charcoal. If weather permits, open the window while the incense smolders.

Tips:

• If you are missing an herb, and you have sufficient herbs for the incense, you can substitute the essential oil for the herb.

• When using charcoal blocks, light from the side. Keep unused blocks in an airtight case.

• Wait until the charcoal block turns white before you add your incense.

• Censers can be anything that is non-flammable and non-metal, from ceramic bowls to sand to everything in-between.

Formulas

Attract Love #1
The Best Time
Create this incense when the moon is new, waxing or full.

Herbs

2 tsp. Sandalwood
1 tsp. Rose Petals
1 tsp. Jasmine Flowers

Attract Love #2
The Best Time
Create this incense when the moon is new, waxing or full.

Herbs

2 tsp. Lemon Balm
1 tsp. Ginger
1 tsp. Orris Root

Attract A Woman
The Best Time
Create this incense when the moon is new, waxing or full.

Herbs

2 tsp. Patchouly
1 tsp. Lemon Balm
1 tsp. Orris Root
1/2 tsp. Cinnamon

Attract A Man
The Best Time
Create this incense when the moon is new, waxing or full.

Herbs
2 tsp. Rosemary
1 tsp. Lavender
1/2 tsp. Ginger
1/2 tsp. Orris Root

Strengthen A Love #1
The Best Time
Create this incense when the moon is waxing or full.

Herbs
2 tsp. Sandalwood
1 tsp. Basil
1 tsp. Mugwort
1 tsp. Rose Petals

Strengthen A Love #2
The Best Time
Create this incense when the moon is waxing or full.

Herbs
1 tsp. Rosemary
1 tsp. Dragon's Blood
1/2 tsp. Cinnamon
1/2 tsp. Basil

Remove Negative Vibrations #1
The Best Time
Create this incense when the moon is waning.

Herbs
1 tsp. Frankincense
1 tsp. Myrrh
1 tsp. Dragon's Blood
1/2 tsp. Fern

Remove Negative Vibrations #2
The Best Time
Create this incense when the moon is waning.

Herbs
2 tsp. Sandalwood
1 tsp. Rosemary
2 Bay Leaves

Protect Your Space From Unwanted Energy
The Best Time
Create this incense when the moon is full.

Herbs
1 tsp. Frankincense
1 tsp. Myrrh
1/2 tsp. Dragon's Blood
1/2 tsp. Juniper
1 Bay Leaf

Find The Courage To Love
The Best Time
Create this incense when the moon is waxing or full.

Herbs
2 tsp. Lavender
2 tsp. Rosemary
1 tsp. Thyme

Boost Your Sex Life #1
The Best Time
Create this incense when the moon is new, waxing or full.

Herbs
1 tsp. Rosemary
1 tsp. Patchouly
1/2 tsp. Chili Pepper
1 Vanilla Bean

Boost Your Sex Life #2
The Best Time
Create this incense when the moon is new, waxing or full.

Herbs
1 tsp. Mint
1 tsp. Cinnamon
1 Vanilla Bean
Pinch of Black Cohosh

Lift A Love Curse #1

The Best Time

Create this incense when the moon is waning.

Herbs

2 tsp. Sandalwood
1 tsp. Nettle
1 tsp. Dragon's Blood

Lift A Love Curse #2

The Best Time

Create this incense when the moon is waning.

Herbs

2 tsp. Rosemary
1 tsp. Rue
1 Bay Leaf

Lift A Love Curse #3

The Best Time

Create this incense when the moon is waning.

Herbs

2 tsp. Sandalwood
1 tsp. Nettle
1 tsp. Rue
1 Bay Leaf

Set The Mood For Love

The Best Time
Create this incense when the moon is new, waxing or full.

Herbs
1 tsp. Rosemary
1 tsp. Rose Petals
1/2 tsp Cinnamon
1/2 tsp. Patchouly
Pinch of Basil

Create A Peaceful And Loving Environment

The Best Time
Create this incense when the moon is new, waxing or full.

Herbs
1 tsp. Rosemary
1 tsp. Lavender
1 tsp. Passion Flower
1/2 tsp. Orris Root

Attract Friendship #1

The Best Time
Create this incense when the moon is new, waxing or full.

Herbs
1 tsp. Frankincense
1 tsp. Rose Petals
1/2 tsp. Catnip
1/2 tsp. Yarrow
Pinch of Orris Root

Attract Friendship #2
The Best Time
Create this incense when the moon is new, waxing or full.

Herbs
1 tsp. Sweetpea
1 tsp. Passion Flower
1/2 tsp. Lemon Peel
1 Bay Leaf
Pinch of Orris Root

Ensure Fidelity From Your Lover
The Best Time
Create this incense when the moon is waxing or full.

Herbs
1 tsp. Basil
1 tsp. Chili Pepper
1 tsp. Cumin
1 slice of dried Rye Bread crumbs
Dash of Lemon Peel

Oils

For centuries, Gypsies have harnessed the magic of essential oils. The aromas are said to lift to the heavens, aiding in the shifting and molding of magical energies.

Oils can be added to magical tools, placed in a diffuser and applied to personal belongings.

You will need a base oil in order to make each different blend.

Base Oils

Almond	Jojoba
Aloe Vera	Olive
Apricot Kernel	Palm
Coconut	Rosehip Seed
Grapeseed	Safflower
Hazelnut	Sunflower

My personal favorite is Jojoba, as it is actually a liquid wax and not oil so it does not get rancid.

Storage

Store away from all sources of heat, light and moisture. **DO NOT STORE IN THE BATHROOM.** It's best to place your oils in dark-colored, airtight glass bottles. and label each for use.

Stones/Crystals

If you cannot obtain the stone(s) listed in the recipe, you can substitute a Clear Quartz Crystal. For extra strength, add a Clear Quartz Crystal with the listed stone. Crystals are natural energizers. Thank the stone/crystal spirit for its help in your quest.

Buying Oils

There are many companies that sell oils. Some are genuine essential oils, extracted from the plants for which they are named, while others are blends or bouquets that are actually a mixture of essential oils to arrive at a certain scent. Many places offer either partially or completely synthetic oils, but most are not labeled as such.

For magic it is best to use the genuine article – essential oils. Since they contain the magical essence of the plant, they are the most favorable way to go.

A good way to tell the difference between synthetic and essential oil is price. Essential oils are expensive, but their potency and ultimate success make them well worth the price.

Making The Oils

1. Place your base oil and essentials oils within reach.
2. Begin by visualizing your need or goal.
3. Once it is clearly formed in your mind, add the base oil to the jar.
4. Add the ingredients in one by one, swirling the jar clockwise to mix. Note how each ingredient affects the aroma of the oil.
5. Take your stone/crystal and place it in your projective hand.
6. Visualize your need or goal.
7. Once it has been clearly formed in your mind, pour your need into the stone/crystal.
8. Add the stone/crystal to the oils.
9. Seal the jar.
10. Store for three days (or at least overnight) before your first use.

Formulas

Attract Love #1

The Best Time
Create this oil when the moon is new, waxing or full.

Supplies
1/8 cup Base Oil
7 drops Rosemary
5 drops Palmarosa
3 drops Lavender
1 tsp. Orris Root, powdered
1 Tiny Rose Quartz
1 Sterilized Glass jar w/ lid

Uses
- Anoint yourself with a few drops on the neck, wrists and ankles.
- Anoint candles.
- Anoint stones/crystals.
- Place a few drops on a cotton ball or handkerchief and inhale when needed.
- Add six to ten drops in your bathwater.
- Place a couple of drops in a diffuser.

Attract Love #2

The Best Time

Create this oil when the moon is new, waxing or full.

Supplies

1/8 cup Base Oil
7 drops Rose
5 drops Cardamom
2 drops Ginger
1 Tiny Amethyst
1 Sterilized Glass jar w/ lid

Uses

- Anoint yourself with a few drops on the neck, wrists and ankles.
- Anoint candles.
- Anoint stones/crystals.
- Place a few drops on a cotton ball or handkerchief and inhale when needed.
- Add six to ten drops in your bathwater.
- Place a couple of drops in a diffuser.

Attract A Woman #1

The Best Time

Create this oil when the moon is new, waxing or full.

Supplies

1/8 cup Base Oil
5 drops Patchouly
3 drops Palmarosa
2 drops Rosemary
1 drop Ginger
1 tsp. Orris Root, powdered
1 Tiny Amethyst
1 Sterilized Glass jar w/ lid

Uses

- Anoint yourself with a few drops on the neck, wrists and ankles.
- Anoint candles.
- Anoint stones/crystals.
- Place a few drops on a cotton ball or handkerchief and inhale when needed.
- Add six to ten drops in your bathwater.
- Place a couple of drops in a diffuser.

Attract A Woman #2

The Best Time

Create this oil when the moon is new, waxing or full.

Supplies

1/8 cup Base Oil
7 drops Ylang-Ylang
5 drops Palmarosa
3 drops Rosemary
2 drops Ginger
1 Tiny Rose Quartz
1 Sterilized Glass jar w/ lid

Uses

- Anoint yourself with a few drops on the neck, wrists and ankles.
- Anoint candles.
- Anoint stones/crystals.
- Place a few drops on a cotton ball or handkerchief and inhale when needed.
- Add six to ten drops in your bathwater.
- Place a couple of drops in a diffuser.

Attract A Man #1
The Best Time
Create this oil when the moon is new, waxing or full.

Supplies
1/8 cup Base Oil
7 drops Rosemary
5 drops Palmarosa
3 drops Geranium
1 drop Vanilla Absolute
1 Tiny Rose Quartz
1 Sterilized Glass jar w/ lid

Uses
- Anoint yourself with a few drops on the neck, wrists and ankles.
- Anoint candles.
- Anoint stones/crystals.
- Place a few drops on a cotton ball or handkerchief and inhale when needed.
- Add six to ten drops in your bathwater.
- Place a couple of drops in a diffuser.

Attract A Man #2

The Best Time

Create this oil when the moon is new, waxing or full.

Supplies

1/8 cup Base Oil
7 drops Lavender
5 drops Palmarosa
3 drops Freesia
1 drop Rose
1 Tiny Clear Quartz Crystal
1 Sterilized Glass jar w/ lid

Uses

• Anoint yourself with a few drops on the neck, wrists and ankles.
• Anoint candles.
• Anoint stones/crystals.
• Place a few drops on a cotton ball or handkerchief and inhale
  when needed.
• Add six to ten drops in your bathwater.
• Place a couple of drops in a diffuser.

Attract A Non-Committed Relationship

The Best Time

Create this oil when the moon is new, waxing or full.

Supplies

1/8 cup Base Oil
6 drops Ylang-Ylang
3 drops Black Pepper
3 drops Cardamom
1 drop Ginger
1 tsp. Orris Root, powdered
1 Tiny Carnelian
1 Sterilized Glass jar w/ lid

Uses

- Anoint yourself with a few drops on the neck, wrists and ankles.
- Anoint candles.
- Anoint stones/crystals.
- Place a few drops on a cotton ball or handkerchief and inhale when needed.
- Add six to ten drops in your bathwater.
- Place a couple of drops in a diffuser.

Boost Sex Life #1

The Best Time

Create this oil when the moon is new, waxing or full.

Supplies

1/8 cup Base Oil
6 drops Ylang-Ylang
3 drops Rose
3 drops Sandalwood
1 drop Ginger
1 Tiny Carnelian
1 Sterilized Glass jar w/ lid

Uses

- Anoint yourself with a few drops on the neck, wrists and ankles.
- Anoint candles.
- Anoint stones/crystals.
- Place a few drops on a cotton ball or handkerchief and inhale when needed.
- Add six to ten drops in your bathwater.
- Place a couple of drops in a diffuser.

Boost Sex Life #2
The Best Time
Create this oil when the moon is new, waxing or full.

Supplies
1/8 cup Base Oil
7 drops Patchouly
5 drops Sandalwood
3 drops Jasmine
1 drop Cardamom
1 Tiny Carnelian
1 Sterilized Glass jar w/ lid

Uses
- Anoint yourself with a few drops on the neck, wrists and ankles.
- Anoint candles.
- Anoint stones/crystals.
- Place a few drops on a cotton ball or handkerchief and inhale when needed.
- Add six to ten drops in your bathwater.
- Place a couple of drops in a diffuser.

Calm Emotions

The Best Time

Create this oil when the moon is full.

Supplies

1/8 cup Base Oil
7 drops Lavender
3 drops Rosemary
3 drops Sandalwood
1 drop Neroli
1 Tiny Amethyst or Malachite
1 Sterilized Glass jar w/ lid

Uses

- Anoint yourself with a few drops on the neck, wrists and ankles.
- Anoint candles.
- Anoint stones/crystals.
- Place a few drops on a cotton ball or handkerchief and inhale when needed.
- Add six to ten drops in your bathwater.
- Place a couple of drops in a diffuser.

Recover From A Broken Heart

The Best Time
Create this oil when the moon is full.

Supplies
1/8 cup Base Oil
6 drops Cypress
4 drops Bergamot
3 drops Jasmine
1 drop Ginger
1 Tiny Amethyst
1 Sterilized Glass jar w/ lid

Uses
- Anoint yourself with a few drops on the neck, wrists and ankles.
- Anoint candles.
- Anoint stones/crystals.
- Place a few drops on a cotton ball or handkerchief and inhale when needed.
- Add six to ten drops in your bathwater.
- Place a couple of drops in a diffuser.

Give Yourself A Surge Of Courage

The Best Time

Create this oil when the moon is new, waxing or full.

Supplies

1/8 cup Base Oil
4 drops Ginger
2 drops Black Pepper
1 drop Clary Sage
1 drop Rosemary
1 Tiny Aquamarine or Bloodstone
1 Sterilized Glass jar w/ lid

Uses

- Anoint yourself with a few drops on the neck, wrists and ankles.
- Anoint candles.
- Anoint stones/crystals.
- Place a few drops on a cotton ball or handkerchief and inhale when needed.
- Add six to ten drops in your bathwater.
- Place a couple of drops in a diffuser.

Date Energy

The Best Time

Create this oil when the moon is new, waxing or full.

Supplies

1/8 cup Base Oil
4 drops Patchouly
3 drops Orange
2 drop Jasmine
1 drop Ginger
1 Tiny Tiger's-Eye
1 Sterilized Glass jar w/ lid

Uses

- Anoint yourself with a few drops on the neck, wrists and ankles.
- Anoint candles.
- Anoint stones/crystals.
- Place a few drops on a cotton ball or handkerchief and inhale when needed.
- Add six to ten drops in your bathwater.
- Place a couple of drops in a diffuser.

Open Yourself Up To Receive Love

The Best Time

Create this oil when the moon is new, waxing or full.

Supplies

1/8 cup Base Oil
6 drops Ylang-Ylang
4 drops Orange
2 drops Jasmine
1 drop Eucalyptus
1 Tiny Amethyst
1 Sterilized Glass jar w/ lid

Uses

- Anoint yourself with a few drops on the neck, wrists and ankles.
- Anoint candles.
- Anoint stones/crystals.
- Place a few drops on a cotton ball or handkerchief and inhale when needed.
- Add six to ten drops in your bathwater.
- Place a couple of drops in a diffuser.

Attract A Spiritual Love
The Best Time
Create this oil when the moon is new, waxing or full.

Supplies
1/8 cup Base Oil
6 drops Lavender
4 drops Sandalwood
2 drops Rosemary
1 tsp. Orris Root, powdered
1 Tiny Amethyst or Moonstone
1 Sterilized Glass jar w/ lid

Uses
• Anoint yourself with a few drops on the neck, wrists and ankles.
• Anoint candles.
• Anoint stones/crystals.
• Place a few drops on a cotton ball or handkerchief and inhale when needed.
• Add six to ten drops in your bathwater.
• Place a couple of drops in a diffuser.

Love And Peace
The Best Time
Create this oil when the moon is new, waxing or full.

Supplies
1/8 cup Base Oil
4 drops Lemon
2 drops Sandalwood
2 drops Jasmine
1 drop Camphor
1 Tiny Aquamarine, Moonstone or Clear Quartz Crystal
1 Sterilized Glass jar w/ lid

Uses
• Anoint yourself with a few drops on the neck, wrists and ankles.
• Anoint candles.
• Anoint stones/crystals.
• Place a few drops on a cotton ball or handkerchief and inhale when needed.
• Place a couple of drops in a diffuser.

Strength, Healing And Protection
The Best Time
Create this oil when the moon is full.

Supplies
1/8 cup Base Oil
4 drops Bergamot
2 drops Juniper
1 drop Orange
1 drop Rosemary
1 Tiny Carnelian, Tiger's-Eye or Clear Quartz Crystal
1 Sterilized Glass jar w/ lid

Uses
- Anoint yourself with a few drops on the neck, wrists and ankles.
- Anoint candles.
- Anoint stones/crystals.
- Place a few drops on a cotton ball or handkerchief and inhale when needed.
- Add six to ten drops in your bathwater.
- Place a couple of drops in a diffuser.

Love And Friendship
The Best Time
Create this oil when the moon is new, waxing or full.

Supplies
1/8 cup Base Oil
5 drops Cardamom
3 drops Freesia
2 drops Geranium
1 drop Palmarosa
1 Tiny Azurite, Lapis Lazuli or Turquoise
1 Sterilized Glass jar w/ lid

Uses
- Anoint yourself with a few drops on the neck, wrists and ankles.
- Anoint candles.
- Anoint stones/crystals.
- Place a few drops on a cotton ball or handkerchief and inhale when needed.
- Add six to ten drops in your bathwater.
- Place a couple of drops in a diffuser.

Love, Healing And Purification

The Best Time

Create this oil when the moon is new, waxing or full.

Supplies

1/8 cup Base Oil
6 drops Freesia
5 drops Cardamom
3 drop Gardenia
2 drops Sandalwood
1 drop Jasmine
1 Tiny Aquamarine, Moonstone or Clear Quartz Crystal
1 Sterilized Glass jar w/ lid

Uses

• Anoint yourself with a few drops on the neck, wrists and ankles.
• Anoint candles.
• Anoint stones/crystals.
• Place a few drops on a cotton ball or handkerchief and inhale when needed.
• Add six to ten drops in your bathwater.
• Place a couple of drops in a diffuser.

Banishment Of Unwanted Energy

The Best Time

Create this oil when the moon is waning.

Supplies

1/8 cup Base Oil
4 drops Juniper
2 drops Black Pepper
1 drop Pine
1 drop Vetivert
1 Tiny Black Tourmaline or Onyx
1 Sterilized Glass jar w/ lid

Uses

- Anoint yourself with a few drops on the neck, wrists and ankles.
- Anoint candles.
- Anoint stones/crystals.
- Place a few drops on a cotton ball or handkerchief and inhale when needed.
- Add six to ten drops in your bathwater.
- Place a couple of drops in a diffuser.

Protection

The Best Time

Create this oil when the moon is full.

Supplies

1/8 cup Base Oil
5 drops Geranium
3 drops Black Pepper
2 drops Juniper
2 drops Peppermint
1 Tiny Tiger's-Eye, Black Agate or Banded Agate
1 Sterilized Glass jar w/ lid

Uses

* Anoint yourself with a few drops on the neck, wrists and ankles.
* Anoint candles.
* Anoint stones/crystals.
* Place a few drops on a cotton ball or handkerchief and inhale when needed.
* Add six to ten drops in your bathwater.
* Place a couple of drops in a diffuser.

Sachets

Sitting around the family fire, gypsies mix together herbs and stones with other objects and tie them up in parcels of cloth. Magical sachets – also known as charms, amulets or talismans – can ward off certain energies or attract a specific energy to you. They can be worn or carried as a personal energy enhancer, or placed in your home to energize your living space.

Material For Sachets

If at all possible, use natural fiber material such as cotton, wool or felt. Same goes for the cord; wool yarn or cotton thread/twine ribbons are ideal materials to use, as synthetic materials seem to interfere with the herbal magic.

The size of the cloth used for a personal sachet should be smaller than one used for the home. Where there's a bigger area to cover then you need more material, i.e. a bigger cloth. I personally like to use cloth pouches – everything fits in nice and neat.

Making Sachets

1. Add each herb into your bowl.
2. Visualize your need or goal.
3. Once it has been clearly formed in your mind, using your projective hand (right if right-handed) mix the herbs as the images from your mind transfer down your arm, through your hand and empower the herbs.
4. Take your stone/crystal and place it in your projective hand.
5. Visualize your need or goal.
6. Once it has been clearly formed in your mind, pour your need into the stone/crystal.
7. Thank the stone/crystal spirit for its help in your quest.
8. Place the herbs and the stone/crystal in the pouch or tie in cloth.

A Clear Quartz Crystal may be substituted for any stone.

Using Sachets

To activate: Hold the sachet in your hand, squeezing gently to release its fragrance. Carry it with you at all times or place in the appropriate spot.

Three months to the date it was made, bury the herbs and continue to use your sachet to hold your crystal/stone.

Formulas

Bring Love To You #1
The Best Time
Create this sachet when the moon is new, waxing or full.

Supplies Needed
3 Tbsp. Lavender
2 Tbsp. Rose Petals
1 Tbsp. Jasmine Flowers
1 Tbsp. Orris Root
1 Rose Quartz
1 Non-metal bowl
1 Pink or Red Pouch or Cloth
1 Thread/Ribbon if Cloth used

Bring Love To You #2
The Best Time
Create this sachet when the moon is new, waxing or full.

Supplies Needed
3 Tbsp. Rose Petals
1 Tbsp. Orange Peel
1 Tbsp. Lemon Peel
1 Tbsp. Geranium
1 Tbsp. High John the Conqueror (poison)
1 Moonstone
1 Non-metal bowl
1 Pink or Red Pouch or Cloth
1 Thread/Ribbon if Cloth used

To Attract A Spicy Love

The Best Time

Create this sachet when the moon is new, waxing or full.

Supplies Needed

3 Tbsp. Rose Petals
2 Tbsp. Chili Pepper
1 Tbsp. Clove
1 Tbsp. Gardenia
1 Beryl
1 Non-metal bowl
1 Red Pouch or Cloth
1 Thread/Ribbon if Cloth used

To Attract A Woman

The Best Time

Create this sachet when the moon is new, waxing or full.

Supplies Needed

3 Tbsp. Rose Petals
2 Tbsp. Catnip
2 Tbsp. Lemon Balm
1 Tbsp. Vetivert
1 Amethyst
1 Non-metal bowl
1 Pink or Red Pouch or Cloth
1 Thread/Ribbon if Cloth used

To Attract A Man
The Best Time
Create this sachet when the moon is new, waxing or full.

Supplies Needed
3 Tbsp. Lavender
2 Tbsp. Gardena Flowers
1 Tbsp. Orange Peel
1 Tbsp. Vetivert
1 Emerald or Amethyst
1 Non-metal bowl
1 Pink or Red Pouch or Cloth
1 Thread/Ribbon if Cloth used

To Attract A Specific Lover
The Best Time
Create this sachet when the moon is new, waxing or full.

Supplies Needed
2 Tbsp. Lemon Verbena
2 Tbsp. Apple Flowers
1 Tbsp. Rose Petals
1 Tbsp. Myrtle
1 Tbsp. Orris Root
1 Strand of the person's hair (or something that belongs to him/her). If nothing is available to you, then write his/her name on a small piece of paper with red/pink ink.
1 Clear Quartz Crystal
1 Non-metal bowl
1 Pink or Red Pouch or Cloth
1 Thread/Ribbon if Cloth used

To Give Your Sex Life A Boost #1
The Best Time
Create this sachet when the moon is new, waxing or full.

Supplies Needed
2 Tbsp. Patchouly
1 Tbsp. Dragons Blood
1 Tbsp. Black Cohosh
1 Tbsp. Ginger
1 Tbsp. Juniper
1 Carnelian
1 Non-metal bowl
1 Red Pouch or Cloth
1 Thread/Ribbon if Cloth used

To Give Your Sex Life A Boost #2
The Best Time
Create this sachet when the moon is new, waxing or full.

Supplies Needed
2 Tbsp. Perinkle
2 Tbsp. Violet
2 Tbsp. Mugwort
1 Tbsp. Lavender
1 Tbsp. Lemongrass
1 Carnelian
1 Non-metal bowl
1 Red Pouch or Cloth
1 Thread/Ribbon if Cloth used

To Decrease Your Sexual Urges
The Best Time
Create this sachet when the moon is waning.

Supplies Needed
4 Tbsp. Camphor
2 Tbsp. Vervain
2 Tbsp. Witch Hazel
1 Aquamarine
1 Non-metal bowl
1 Black or White Pouch or Cloth
1 Thread/Ribbon if Cloth used

To Accept And Love Yourself
The Best Time
Create this sachet when the moon is new, waxing or full.

Supplies Needed
3 Tbsp. Lavender
2 Tbsp. Rosemary
2 Tbsp. Gardenia
1 Tbsp. Pink Geranium
1 Amethyst
1 Non-metal bowl
1 Pink Pouch or Cloth
1 Thread/Ribbon if Cloth used

To Encourage A Marriage Proposal
The Best Time
Create this sachet when the moon is new, waxing or full.

Supplies Needed
3 Tbsp. Apple Flowers
2 Tbsp. Orris Root
2 Adam & Eve Roots
1 Lucky Hand
1 Sardonyx
1 Non-metal bowl
1 Pink or Red Pouch or Cloth
1 Thread/Ribbon if Cloth used

To Encourage An Amicable Separation
The Best Time
Create this sachet when the moon is full.

Supplies Needed
3 Tbsp. Buckthorn
2 Tbsp. Comfrey
2 Tbsp. Mugwort
1 Tbsp. Betony, Wood
1 Solomon's Seal
1 Amethyst or Kunzite
1 Non-metal bowl
1 Light Blue or Indigo Pouch or Cloth
1 Thread/Ribbon if Cloth used

To Attract Friendship

The Best Time

Create this sachet when the moon is new, waxing or full.

Supplies Needed

3 Tbsp. Passion Flower
2 Tbsp. Sweetpea
1 Tbsp. Lemon Peel
1 Tbsp. Orange Peel
1 Turquoise or Pink Tourmaline
1 Non-metal bowl
1 Pink or Green Pouch or Cloth
1 Thread/Ribbon if Cloth used

To Heal A Friendship

The Best Time

Create this sachet when the moon is waxing or full.

Supplies Needed

3 Tbsp. Lavender
2 Tbsp. St. John Wort (poison)
2 Tbsp. Passion Flower
1 Tbsp. Rosemary
1 Amethyst
1 Non-metal bowl
1 Pink or Yellow Pouch or Cloth
1 Thread/Ribbon if Cloth used

To Heal A Lovers Quarrel #1

The Best Time
Create this sachet when the moon is waxing or full.

Supplies Needed
3 Tbsp. Lavender
2 Tbsp. Carnation
1 Tbsp. St. John's Wort (poison)
1 Tbsp. Lemon Balm
1 Moonstone
1 Non-metal bowl
1 Light Blue or White Pouch or Cloth
1 Thread/Ribbon if Cloth used

To Heal A Lovers Quarrel #2

The Best Time
Create this sachet when the moon is waxing or full.

Supplies Needed
3 Tbsp. Lavender
2 Tbsp. Rosemary
1 Tbsp. Jasmine Flower
1 Tbsp. Cinnamon
1 Chrysocolla
1 Non-metal bowl
1 Light Blue or White Pouch or Cloth
1 Thread/Ribbon if Cloth used

To Protect You From Unwanted Attention Or Energy

The Best Time

Create this sachet when the moon is full or waning.

Supplies Needed

3 Tbsp. Carnation

2 Tbsp. Huckleberry

2 Tbsp. Vervain

1 Tbsp. Chili Pepper

1 Black Tourmaline

1 Non-metal bowl

1 White Pouch or Cloth

1 Thread/Ribbon if Cloth used

To Strengthen A Relationship

The Best Time

Create this sachet when the moon is new, waxing or full.

Supplies Needed

3 Tbsp. Lavender

2 Tbsp. Pennyroyal

2 Tbsp. Carnation

2 Tbsp. Rose Petals

1 Bay Leaf

1 Turquoise

1 Non-metal bowl

1 Pink or Red Pouch or Cloth

1 Thread/Ribbon if Cloth used

To Help Encourage A Love To Grow

The Best Time
Create this sachet when the moon is new, waxing or full.

Supplies Needed
2 Tbsp. Lavender
2 Tbsp. Rose Petals & Hips
1 Tbsp. Rosemary
1 Tbsp. Pimento
1 slice of dried Rye Bread crumbs
1 Moonstone
1 Non-metal bowl
1 Pink or Red Pouch or Cloth
1 Thread/Ribbon if Cloth used

To Mend A Broken Heart

The Best Time
Create this sachet when the moon is full.

Supplies Needed
3 Tbsp. Lemon Balm
2 Tbsp. Rosemary
2 Tbsp. Rose Petals
1 Tbsp. Cinnamon
1 Amethyst
1 Non-metal bowl
1 Light Blue or White Pouch or Cloth
1 Thread/Ribbon if Cloth used

Spells

Whether around the campfire, in their caravan or in the home of a new acquaintance, spells are a gypsy's best friend. A combination of magical tools, powerful words and strong intentions, spells can create or repel any goal...at any time.

Because a spellcaster must feel at ease when casting a spell, use parts of the spells that make you feel comfortable and ignore the ones that do not.

Spells are very personal, very "me" oriented and because of that I encourage you to make any changes to the spells to fit you. Subtract oils, add herbs, rework words – it does not matter as long as it works for you.

Attract A Lover

The Best Time
Cast this spell when the moon is new, waxing or full.

The Best Day
Friday

Incense To Use (choose one)
Frankincense, Rosemary, Attract Love #1 or #2, Attract a Woman, Attract a Man

Herbs To Use
Powdered Sugar

Oils To Use (choose one)
Vanilla Absolute, Attract Love #1 or #2, Attract a Women #1 or #2, Attract a Man #1 or #2

Candles To Use
One White, One Pink, One Orange

Stones To Use
None

Other Supplies Needed
Three Candleholders, One Fireproof Bowl (non-metal), One Charcoal Block

Preparation
- Gather supplies
- Carve "Your Name" into the WHITE candle, "Love" into the PINK candle, and "Attraction" into the ORANGE candle.
- Place each candle into your projective hand (right if right handed – left if left handed) to empower it. Visualize your need; feel the emotions associated with it. Once you can no

longer hold the image or feel the emotions, then the energy has moved from you into the candle. Empower "You" into WHITE candle, "Friendship" into the PINK candle, and "Stimulation" into the ORANGE candle.

- Anoint ALL CANDLES with the OIL of choice. Starting in the middle of the candle, perform 9 strokes going up, then again starting in the middle of the candle, do 9 strokes going down. Never rub up and then down in the same motion.
- Roll ALL the candles in the POWDERED SUGAR.
- Place candles in their candleholders.

Activation

- Light CHARCOAL BLOCK, place in ONE FIREPROOF BOWL and burn INCENSE.
- Meditate on the desired outcome –clear your mind and focus on what you want to accomplish.

Take the WHITE candle and put it in the middle of your workspace. As you light it, recite:

**Here is (your name),
This candle is me.
I am in search of,
True love and life-long mate.
As the fire burns, so burns my spirit.**

Take the PINK candle, placing it next to the WHITE candle. As you light it, recite:

**The respect and friendship,
I search for
Draws close with this flame.**

**It burns as does the fire draw,
him/her to me and from me to him/her.**

From this moment forward
The love I search for reaches out to me
It holds me,
Caresses me,
Wills me to find it, as I will it to find me.

Finally, take the ORANGE candle and place it next to the WHITE candle. As you light it, recite:

My love feels the pull to find me,
As a nighttime creature flocks to a flame such as this,
The attraction is so great it cannot be resisted,
It draws, it pulls, it attracts,
As it burns, so burns my loves determination to find me.

Meditate on the goal of your love coming to you first as friends, then moving forward with him/her into a loving, committed relationship. Once that goal has been visualized, the energy work has begun.

Let the candles burn down or for at least nine minutes. If you must extinguish the flame, do so with a snuffer as blowing will scatter the energy. Bury the wax.

Help Your Love To Grow And Prosper

The Best Time
Cast this spell when the moon is full.

The Best Day
Friday

Incense To Use (choose one)
Frankincense, Rosemary, Strengthen a Love #1, Strengthen a Love #2

Herbs To Use
None

Oils To Use
None

Candles To Use
None

Stones To Use
One Rose Quartz

Other Supplies Needed
Packet of Flower Seeds, Potting Soil, Pot, Spring Water, One Fireproof Bowl (non-metal), One Charcoal Block

Preparation:
Gather supplies

Activation
- Light CHARCOAL BLOCK, place in ONE FIREPROOF BOWL and burn INCENSE.
- Meditate on the desired outcome –clear your mind and focus on what you want to accomplish.

Place the SOIL into the POT. Put it in the middle of your workspace.

Take your ROSE QUARTZ and ask it for its help and guidance. Touch it to the middle of your forehead and to your heart. Kiss it gently.

Place the Rose Quartz into your projective hand (right if right handed – left if left handed). Visualize the love with your mate growing stronger and becoming the love you desire. Feel the emotions associated with this love. Once you can no longer hold the image or feel the emotions, then the energy has moved from you into the crystal.

Thank the Rose Quartz for its help. Bury the Rose Quartz in the soil.

Take the a few FLOWER SEEDS (depending on the size of your pot). As you plant the seeds over the Rose Quartz, recite:

With these seeds,
Our love shall bloom, grow and prosper.

Water the seeds with the SPRING WATER.
Place the pot into a sunny area. Your love will strengthen as the seeds germinate and the flowers grow.

Once the flowers have lived their life cycle, you may return the plants and the soil to the earth. You can reuse the Rose Quartz and the pot to plant more seeds from the same packet or a new one.

Attract A Healthy Relationship

The Best Time
Cast this spell when the moon is new, waxing or full.

The Best Day
Friday

Incense To Use (choose one)
Frankincense, Strengthen a Love #1, Strengthen a Love #2, Create a Peaceful and Loving Environment

Herbs To Use
Cinnamon and Powder Sugar

Oils To Use (choose one)
Strength-Health-Protection, Lavender

Candles To Use
One Pink

Stones To Use
None

Other Supplies Needed
One Lemon, Nine Straight Pins (any color BUT black), Red or Pink Ribbon, One Candleholder, Two Fireproof Bowls (non-metal), One Charcoal Block

Preparation
- Gather supplies
- In the BOWL, mix together a pinch of CINNAMON and POWDERED SUGAR. Place mixture off to the side.
- Using a straight pin, carve your name and birth date into the LEMON rind. Then, carve "Healthy Love" into the PINK candle.
- Place the PINK candle into your projective hand (right if right handed – left if left handed) to empower it. Visualize a healthy love coming into your life. Feel the emotions associated with this love. Once you

can no longer hold the image or feel the emotions, then the energy has moved from you into the candle. Empower the candle with "You."

- Anoint the candle with the OIL of choice. Starting in the middle of the candle, perform 9 strokes going up, then again starting in the middle of the candle, do 9 strokes going down. Never rub up and then down in the same motion.
- Roll the candle in the HERBAL MIXTURE.
- Place candle in its candleholder.

Activation

- Light CHARCOAL BLOCK, place in ONE FIREPROOF BOWL and burn INCENSE.
- Meditate on the desired outcome –clear your mind and focus on what you want to accomplish.

Light the PINK candle and place it in the middle of your workspace.

Next, take the LEMON and the nine PINS. Place one pin through the top, leaving enough room to tie the thread/ribbon onto the head. Starting on one side, place the pins into the lemon, diagonally, alternating sides until finished. As you place the pins in the lemon, recite:

I make a promise to myself to attract a healthy relationship.
One that will attract positive energy that is full of love and long lasting.

Tie the THREAD/RIBBON to the head of the top pin.
Place the lemon in front of the candle.

Stare into the candle's flame. Meditate on the goal of attracting a healthy relationship. Once that goal is visualized, the energy work has begun.

Let the candles burn down or for at least nine minutes. If you must extinguish the flame, do so with a snuffer as blowing will scatter the energy. Bury the wax.

ang the lemon in a window – replace when needed or remove when love arrives.

Encourage An Offer Of Marriage

The Best Time
Cast this spell when the moon is waxing or full.

The Best Day
Friday

Incense To Use (choose one)
Frankincense, Rosemary, Strengthen a Love #1, Strengthen a Love #2

Herbs To Use
None

Oils To Use (choose one)
Love- Healing-Purification, Lavender

Candles To Use
One White, One Black

Stones To Use
None

Other Supplies Needed
Red Thread or Ribbon, Two Fireproof Bowls (non-metal), One Charcoal Block

Preparation:
- Carve "Your Name" into WHITE candle and "Your Partner's Name" into the BLACK candle.
- Place each candle into your projective hand (right if right handed – left if left handed) to empower it. Visualize your need, feeling the emotions associated with it. Once you can no longer hold the image or feel the emotions, then the energy has moved from you into the candle. Empower "You"

into WHITE candle and "Your Partner" into the BLACK candle.

- Anoint the candle with the OIL of choice. Starting in the middle of the candle, perform 9 strokes going up, then again starting in the middle of the candle, do 9 strokes going down. Never rub up and then down in the same motion.
- Place candles in their candleholders.

Activation

- Light CHARCOAL BLOCK, place in ONE FIREPROOF BOWL and burn INCENSE.
- Meditate on the desired outcome –clear your mind and focus on what you want to accomplish.

Visualize your beloved proposing marriage as you tie the TWO CANDLES together with the THREAD/RIBBON.

Slightly melt the bottom of the CANDLES over the BOWL. Place the candle into the bowl – they should be able to stand on their own.

Visualize the two of you at your wedding. Once the image is held in your mind recite:

> **Do you (Your Name) take (Partner's Name) to have and to hold, to honor, cherish and love until death do you part? Yes!**

> **Do you (Partner's Name) take (Your Name) to have and to hold, to honor, cherish and love until death do you part? Yes!**

> **I now pronounce you husband and wife. You may kiss your bride.**

Let the candles burn until finished.

Keep the melted wax in your underwear drawer until the question is asked. Bury the wax after the proposal.

End A Relationship

The Best Time
Cast this spell when the moon is full or waning.

The Best Day
Monday or Friday

Incense To Use (choose one)
Frankincense, Rosemary, Remove Negative Vibrations #1, Remove Negative Vibrations #2

Herbs To Use
Salt

Oils To Use (choose one)
Banishment of Unwanted Energy, Olive

Candles To Use
Black

Stones To Use
None

Other Supplies Needed
A picture of you two as a couple, Pen or Marker, Tweezers, Two Fireproof Bowls (non-metal), Scissors, One Charcoal Block

Preparation:
- Carve "Your Name" and "Your Partner's Name" into the BLACK candle.
- Place each candle into your projective hand (right if right handed – left if left handed) to empower it. Visualize your need; feel the emotions associated with it. Once you can no longer hold the image or feel the emotions, then the energy has moved from you into the candle. Empower "You", "Your Partner" and the break-up of your relationship into the BLACK candle.

- Anoint the candle with the OIL of choice. Starting in the middle of the candle, perform 9 strokes going up, then again starting in the middle of the candle, do 9 strokes going down. Never rub up and then down in the same motion.

Activation

- Light CHARCOAL BLOCK, place in ONE FIREPROOF BOWL and burn INCENSE.
- Meditate on the desired outcome – clear your mind and focus on what you want to accomplish.

Place the BLACK candle in the center of the BOWL. Pour SALT around the base of the candle so that it will stand on its own. Place the bowl in the middle of your workspace.

Light the BLACK candle and visualize all of the reasons you wish for the relationship to end. Do not think negative, hateful thoughts, but instead think of all of the positive reasons for this relationship to come to a close. As the candle melts away, the salt will absorb the wax; as it does so, imagine that your relationship is being absorbed into the earth (salt) and being neutralized right there before you.

Take the MARKER and place an "X" through the center of the PICTURE.

Next, grab your SCISSORS. As you cut the picture in half, so that you two are separate, recite:

> **What was once together,**
> **Is now in two,**
> **The passion (Your partner's name) had for me**
> **Is now gone and I am free.**

Grab and hold a piece of the PICTURE with the TWEEZERS over the flame. Let the ashes fall into the bowl. Repeat procedure with the other half. Once cooled, bury the ashes and the wax/salt lump.

Keep Your Lover Faithful

The Best Time
Cast this spell when the moon is waxing or full.

The Best Day
Thursday or Friday

Incense To Use (choose one)
Frankincense, Rosemary, Ensure Fidelity from Your Lover

Herbs To Use
Two chili peppers or ground chili pepper*

Oils To Use
None

Candles To Use
None

Stones To Use
None

Other Supplies Needed
Two Red or Pink Ribbon/Threads, Partner's Sexual Fluid and/or Pubic Hair**, Jar with Lid, Pair of Your Dirty Underwear, One Fireproof Bowl (non-metal), One Charcoal Block

Preparation:
- Offer your partner a cloth to clean himself/herself with after sex. Reserve the cloth. Do not get any of your sexual fluids on this cloth!
- Gather supplies.

*If you use the chili powder, sprinkle it directly onto the cloth.
** If you cannot obtain your partner's sexual fluids, a lock of hair and/or article of clothing will do.

Activation

• Light CHARCOAL BLOCK, place in ONE FIREPROOF BOWL and burn INCENSE.

• Meditate on the desired outcome – clear your mind and focus on what you want to accomplish.

Tie the CHILI PEPPERS together with the one THREAD/RIBBON. Place the CHILI PEPPERS into the CLOTH and place your UNDERWEAR on top of the peppers.

Roll up the CLOTH. Take the second THREAD/RIBBON. As you tie it around the rolled cloth recite:

**With this wrap
You will in fact
Stay out of the sack
With anyone else but me.**

Stuff the tied bundle into the JAR. Seal the jar tight.

Bury the jar. Walk away from it without looking back.

Recover From A Broken Heart

The Best Time
Cast this spell when the moon is full.

The Best Day
Sunday

Incense To Use (choose one)
Frankincense, Rosemary, Remove Negative Vibrations #1,
Remove Negative Vibrations #2, Create a Peaceful and Loving
Environment

Herbs To Use
Cloves

Oils To Use (choose one)
Recover from a Broken Heart, Eucalyptus

Candles To Use
One Pink, Two Blue

Stones To Use
Three Amethysts, Three Rose Quartz

Other Supplies Needed
Three Candleholders, Camomile Tea, A Cloth Pouch or Sachet,
An Object to Grind Herb, One Fireproof Bowl (non-metal), One
Charcoal Block

Preparation
- Gather supplies
- Prepare CAMOMILE TEA
- Grind CLOVES into a powder
- Carve "Your Name" into the PINK candle, "Peace" into the
  BLUE candles.

- Place the each candle into your projective hand (right if right handed – left if left handed) to empower it. Visualize your need; feel the emotions associated with it. Once you can no longer hold the image or feel the emotions, then the energy has moved from you into the candle. Empower "You" into PINK candle, "Healing" into the BLUE candles.
- Anoint ALL CANDLES with the OIL of choice, using 9 strokes starting in the middle of the candle, going up, then starting in the middle of the candle, and 9 strokes going down. Never rub up and then down in the same motion.
- Roll ALL the candles in the CLOVE powder.
- Place candles in their candleholders.
- Sip on your CAMOMILE TEA throughout this spell.

Activation
- Light CHARCOAL BLOCK, place in ONE FIREPROOF BOWL and burn INCENSE.
- Meditate on the desired outcome – clear your mind and focus on what you want to accomplish.

Take the PINK candle it a candleholder. Put it in the middle of your workspace. As you light it, recite:

> **Here is (your name),**
> **This candle is me.**
> **As the fire burns, so burns my spirit.**

Take your three AMETHYSTS and ROSE QUARTZ in your hands and ask them for their help and guidance. Touch them to the middle of your forehead and to your heart. Kiss them each gently.

Place the stones onto your workstation. projective hand (right if right handed – left if left handed) and put it over the stones. Visualize your heart healing with love and peace entering your life. Feel the emotions associated. Once you can no longer hold the image or feel the emotions, then the energy has moved from you into the stones.

Thank the stones for their help. Starting at noon and going clockwise, place them around the PINK candle, alternating the AMETHYSTS and ROSE QUARTZ. (A, RQ, A, RQ, A, RQ). As you place then recite:

In these rocks, I will lock
My faith that my heart will mend
And that the Divine will send
Another to share my life.

Take the BLUE candles. Place these candles outside the CIRCLE OF STONES and one to the left and the other to the right of the PINK candle. As you light them, recite:

The bonds of yesteryear,
No longer hold me dear.
As I release my anger, loss and pain,
My heart and soul is free to love again.

Finish your CHAMOMILE TEA while you stare into the flames and visualize peace, love and healing.

Once the candles burn down, bury the wax. Place the stones into the pouch.

Carry the stones with you. If you find that you need extra support, hold one or more stones in your receptive hand and absorb their light and love.

Encourage Your Lover To Call

The Best Time
Cast this spell when the moon is waxing or full.

The Best Day
Wednesday or Friday

Incense To Use (choose one)
Frankincense, Rosemary, Attract Love #1, Attract Love #2

Herbs To Use
Allspice

Oils To Use
None

Candles To Use
None

Stones To Use
None

Other Supplies Needed
One Picture of You, One Picture of Them (if you do not have a picture, write their name and some personal notes about them on a piece of paper), Paper Clips, Phone, One Fireproof Bowl (non-metal), One Charcoal Block

Preparation
• Gather supplies

Activation
• Light CHARCOAL BLOCK, place in ONE FIREPROOF BOWL and burn INCENSE.

• Meditate on the desired outcome – clear your mind and focus on what you want to accomplish.

Use the PAPER CLIPS to fasten YOUR PHOTO face down to your LOVER'S PHOTO. As you do this recite:

Set (Insert Name) heart on fire
Let him/her feel a great desire
To contact me
For he/she will see
That they will find no peace
Until he/she speaks to me.

Place the PHOTOS under the PHONE.

Visualize him/her picking up the phone and calling you. Feel the excitement of the communication, reciting the conversation in your head. Once you have a good, clear picture of what you wish to happen, the magic has begun.

Do not dwell on the phone call. Do not watch the phone and expect it to ring. Go about your life and the Divine will answer your plea for help.

Discourage A Suitor's Advances

The Best Time
Cast this spell when the moon is full or waning.

The Best Day
Friday

Incense To Use (choose one)
Frankincense, Rosemary, Protect Your Space From Unwanted Energy

Herbs To Use
Salt, Fennel

Oils To Use (choose one)
Banishment, Olive

Candles To Use
Two Black

Stones To Use
None

Other Supplies Needed
One Apple, Eight Pieces of Paper, Pen, One Fireproof Bowl (non-metal), Two Candleholders, One Charcoal Block

Preparation
- Gather supplies
- Carve "Name of Unwanted Suitor" into the BLACK candles.
- Place the each candle into your projective hand (right if right handed – left if left handed) to empower it. Visualize your need; feel the emotions associated with it. Once you can no longer hold the image or feel the emotions, then the energy has moved from you into the candle. Empower "The Suitor Leaving You Alone" into the BLACK candles.

- Anoint ALL CANDLES with the OIL of choice, using 9 strokes starting in the middle of the candle, going up, then starting in the middle of the candle, and 9 strokes going down. Never rub up and then down in the same motion.
- Roll ALL the candles in the SALT.
- Place candles in their candleholders.

Activation

- Light CHARCOAL BLOCK, place in ONE FIREPROOF BOWL and burn INCENSE.
- Meditate on the desired outcome – clear your mind and focus on what you want to accomplish.

Place the BLACK candles in the center of your workspace. In between the candles, place one sheet of PAPER. On that paper, write the UNWANTED SUITOR'S name. Draw a circle around the name and place an "X" through the center.

Squeeze the JUICE of the APPLE over the name. Fold the paper in half four times until you get a small square while you visualize your desire to repeal the suitor.

Place the folded paper in the BOWL and burn. As the paper burns recite:

My heart is free to love who I want
You're not it, not even a bit
Leave me alone, just go away
Don't contact me by phone
Or any other way.

Take the SEVEN PIECES OF PAPER and place an equal share of the paper ash on each. Sprinkle a pinch of FENNEL over each pile of ash. Fold each paper into a small envelope. Drip candle wax onto the paper envelops to seal them – as you do this, do not think any vengeful thoughts.

Bury the envelops in seven separate holes.

Bind Your Lover To You

(Note: REALLY make sure that you want to be bound to this individual forever. Be forewarned – if you do this spell out of spite or with vengeful thoughts, it will come back to bite you in the butt!)

The Best Time
Cast this spell when the moon is waxing or full.

The Best Day
Friday

Incense To Use (choose one)
Frankincense, Rosemary, Strengthen a Love #1, Strengthen a Love #2

Herbs To Use
None

Oils To Use
None

Candles To Use
None

Stones To Use
None

Other Supplies Needed
One Apple, Honey, Three Pieces of Red or Pink Ribbon/Thread of the same length, Stand of Your Hair, Strand of your Lover's Hair, One Fireproof Bowl (non-metal), One Charcoal Block

Preparation
• Gather supplies

Activation

- Light CHARCOAL BLOCK, place in ONE FIREPROOF BOWL and burn INCENSE.
- Meditate on the desired outcome – clear your mind and focus on what you want to accomplish.

Cut the APPLE horizontally so that you can see the star shape inside.

Spread HONEY on both sides.

Place one STRAND of HAIR on each side of the APPLE. Bring both halves together to enclose the hairs.

Take the 3 pieces of RIBBON and braid then together, leaving 1 inch free on either end while you visualize you and your beloved together through all of eternity with this spiritual marriage.

Tie the APPLE together with the BRAID.

Bury the APPLE in a romantic spot – preferably by roses.

Capture The Heart Of The One You Love

The Best Time
Cast this spell when the moon is new, waxing or full.

The Best Day
Friday

Incense To Use (choose one)
Frankincense, Rosemary, Attract Love #1, Attract Love #2, Attract a Woman, Attract a Man

Herbs To Use
Bean Seeds

Oils To Use (choose one)
Love and Friendship, Lavender

Candles To Use
None

Stones To Use
One Rose Quartz

Other Supplies Needed
Potting Soil, Spring Water, Piece of Paper, Pen, One Fireproof Bowl (non-metal), One Charcoal Block

Preparation
- Gather supplies
- Anoint BEANS with OIL of choice.

Activation
- Light CHARCOAL BLOCK, place in ONE FIREPROOF BOWL and burn INCENSE.
- Meditate on the desired outcome – clear your mind and focus on what you want to accomplish.

Place the POTTING SOIL into the POT. Put it in the middle of your workspace.

Take your ROSE QUARTZ and ask it for its help and guidance. Touch it to the middle of your forehead and to your heart. Kiss it gently.

Place the Rose Quartz into your projective hand (right if right handed – left if left handed). Visualize the one you love returning your feelings and you two moving forward to become the couple you desire. Feel the emotions associated with this love. Once you can no longer hold the image or feel the emotions, then the energy has moved from you into the crystal.

Thank the Rose Quartz for its help. Bury the Rose Quartz in the soil.

Take the BEAN SEEDS (depending on the size of your pot). As you plant the seeds over the Rose Quartz, recite:

As these seeds blossom
May (Insert Name) love be returned to me
So that our relationship can prosper and bloom.

Water the seeds with the SPRING WATER.

Place the pot into a sunny area. Your love will strengthen as the seeds germinate and the plants grow.

When the BEANS are at maturity: pick and prepare to personal taste.

Once the plants have lived their life cycle – you may return the plants and the soil to the earth. You can reuse the Rose Quartz and the pot to plant more seeds from that same packet or a new packet.

Ready Yourself For Love

(Note: Before one can attract love, one has to be ready spiritually and emotionally.)

The Best Time
Cast this spell when the moon is new, waxing or full.

The Best Day
Friday

Incense To Use (choose one)
Frankincense, Rosemary, Remove Negativity #1, Remove Negativity #2, Set the Mood for Love, Create a Peaceful and Loving Environment, Find the Courage to Love

Herbs To Use
Powder Sugar

Oils To Use (choose one)
Open Yourself Up to Receive Love, Eucalyptus, Lavender

Candles To Use
One White, Two Pink, Two Blue

Stones To Use (choose one)
Rose Quartz, Clear Quartz Crystal

Other Supplies Needed
If Applicable – Your Ex's Belongings and Trinkets, Your Saliva, Five Candleholders, One Fireproof Bowl (non-metal), One Charcoal Block

Preparation
- Gather supplies
- Toss out all of your ex-lover's belongings. If you can't bear to toss them, then give to a friend or put in storage. But you

MUST get them out of your house! There is no room for the new if the old is still around to remind you of what has been.

- Carve "Your Name" into the WHITE candle, "Love" into the PINK candles, and "Peace" into the BLUE candles.
- Place the each candle into your projective hand (right if right handed – left if left handed) to empower it. Visualize your need; feel the emotions associated with it. Once you can no longer hold the image or feel the emotions, then the energy has moved from you into the candle. Empower "You" into WHITE candle, "Love" into the PINK candles, and "Harmony" into the BLUE candles.
- Anoint the WHITE candle with your SALIVA, ALL OTHER CANDLES with the OIL of choice using 9 strokes starting in the middle of the candle, going up, then starting in the middle of the candle, and 9 strokes going down. Never rub up and then down in the same motion.
- Roll ALL the candles in the POWDER SUGAR.
- Place candles in their candleholders.

Activation
- Light CHARCOAL BLOCK, place in ONE FIREPROOF BOWL and burn INCENSE.
- Meditate on the desired outcome – clear your mind and focus on what you want to accomplish.

Take the WHITE candle it a candleholder. Put it in the middle of your workspace. As you light it, recite:

This flame is (Insert Name)
My soul, my essence
As it burns, so burns my spirit.

Take your ROSE QUARTZ and ask it for its help and guidance. Touch it to the middle of your forehead and to your heart. Kiss it gently.

Place the Rose Quartz into your projective hand (right if right handed – left if left handed). Visualize yourself being open and receptive to love. Feel the emotions associated with this love. Once you can no longer hold the image or feel the emotions, then the energy has moved from you into the stone.

Thank the Rose Quartz for its help and place it next to the WHITE candle.

Take the PINK and BLUE candles. Starting at NOON and going clockwise, place the candles in an alternating fashion around the WHITE candle. In the order you placed the candles, light them. As you light, recite:

Magic circle, infuse my heart with peace and harmony
Open my closed heart to ready me for love
With blessings from above
Let me attract a healthy relationship effortlessly.

Mediate on the goal of your love finding you as friends and then moving forward with him/her into a loving, healthy relationship. Once that goal is visualized, the energy work has begun.

Let the candles burn down or for at least nine minutes. If you must extinguish the flame, do so with a snuffer as blowing will scatter the energy. Bury the wax.

Carry the stone with you. If you find that you need extra support, hold it in your receptive hand and absorb their light and love.

Encourage A Second Chance

The Best Time
Cast this spell when the moon is new, waxing or full.

The Best Day
Wednesday or Friday

Incense To Use (choose one)
Frankincense, Rosemary, Set the Mood for Love, Create a
Peaceful and Loving Environment

Herbs To Use
Bay Leaves, Cinnamon, Powdered Sugar, Star Anises

Oils To Use
None

Candles To Use
One Purple

Stones To Use
None

Other Supplies Needed
Two New Stickpins, One Candleholder, Two Fireproof Bowls
(non-metal), Ex-Lover's Personal Clothing*, One Charcoal Block

Preparation
• Gather supplies
• Carve "Your Lover's Name" into the PURPLE candle.
• Place the candle into your projective hand (right if right
  handed – left if left handed) to empower it. Visualize your need;
  feel the emotions associated with it. Once you can no longer hold
  the image or feel the emotions, then the energy has moved from
  you into the candle. Empower "Your Lover" into PURPLE candle.

- Place candle in its candleholder.

*If you do not have any of his/her clothing, then a gift or picture will do.

Activation
- Light CHARCOAL BLOCK, place in ONE FIREPROOF BOWL and burn INCENSE.
- Meditate on the desired outcome – clear your mind and focus on what you want to accomplish.

Take your two STICK PINS and slide them into the PURPLE CANDLE from right to left and left to right to pick the wick and form a cross. As you place the STICK PINS in recite:

**It's not the candle I wish to stick
But (Insert Name)'s heart I need to prick
No matter if he/she is asleep or awake
Desire will course through his/her body and cause it to quake
Until he/she comes to me and love we make.**

Place the CANDLE in the middle of your workspace and light it.

Take the HERBS and place equal parts into your BOWL. As you mix the HERBS with your projective HAND, recite:

**By this light, I stir my mix
Bring him/her back
And make it quick.**

Sprinkle the HERBAL MIX on your EX-LOVER'S personal clothing, especially his/her underwear or socks. Take the clothes and place in your underwear drawer.

Let the candle burn down and cool. Bury the wax and the pins.

To Make-Up

The Best Time
Cast this spell when the moon is new, waxing or full.

The Best Day
Tuesday, Wednesday or Friday

Incense To Use (choose one)
Frankincense, Rosemary, Remove Negative Vibrations #1,
Remove Negative Vibrations #2, Set the Mood for Love, Create
a Peaceful and Loving Environment

Herbs To Use
Rose Petals, Lavender, Peppermint

Oils To Use
None

Candles To Use
None

Stones To Use
One Moonstone

Other Supplies Needed
Container w/Lid and Powder Puff, Rice Powder, Toenail
Clippings or Strands of Hair from BOTH You and Your Mate*,
One Fireproof Bowl (non-metal), One Charcoal Block

Preparation
• Gather supplies
*If you do not have toenail clipping or hair from your mate,
write his/her name on a piece of paper with a few other
personal remarks.

Activation

- Light CHARCOAL BLOCK, place in ONE FIREPROOF BOWL and burn INCENSE.
- Meditate on the desired outcome – clear your mind and focus on what you want to accomplish.

In your BOWL, add equals amount of ROSE PETAL, LAVENDER and PEPPERMINT. Mix with your projective HAND as you visualize you and your mate making-up.

Take your MOONSTONE and ask it for its help and guidance. Touch it to the middle of your forehead and to your heart. Kiss it gently.

Place the Moonstone into your projective hand (right if right handed – left if left handed). Visualize you and your mate soothing over your troubles and strengthening your mutual love for one another. Feel the emotions associated. Once you can no longer hold the image or feel the emotions, then the energy has moved from you into the stone.

Thank the Moonstone for its assistance and add it to the bowl.

Add YOUR TOENAIL/HAIR and your MATE'S TOENAIL/HAIR to the bowl as you recite:

With my beloved's (Insert Item Used)
And my (Insert Item Used)
I proclaim our feud to end
And our hearts to mend
So that our souls reunite again.

Add enough RICE POWDER to make a mix.

Sprinkle the HERBAL POWDER on your BED and on YOURSELF. If possible, sprinkle some in loved ones clothes drawers. Repeat daily until rift is healed.

Turn A Friendship Into Love

The Best Time
Cast this spell when the moon is new, waxing or full.

The Best Day
Friday

Incense To Use (choose one)
Frankincense, Rosemary, Attract Love #1, Attract Love #2, Attract a Woman, Attract a Man, Set the Mood for Love

Herbs To Use
Lemon (juice), Powder Sugar

Oils To Use
None

Candles To Use
One Red, One Pink

Stones To Use
None

Other Supplies Needed
One Red/Pink Thread or Ribbon, One Piece of Red Cloth. Two Fireproof Bowls (non-metal), One Charcoal Block

Preparation
- Gather supplies
- Carve "Friendship" and "Both of Your Names" into the PINK candle, "Love" and "Both of Your Names" into the RED candle.
- Place each candle into your projective hand (right if right handed – left if left handed) to empower it. Visualize your need; feel the emotions associated with it. Once you can no longer hold the image or feel the emotions, then the energy has moved from you into the candle. Empower "You Two as

Friends" into PINK candle, "You Two as Romantic Partners" into the RED candle.

- Anoint ALL CANDLES with the LEMON OIL, using 9 strokes starting in the middle of the candle, going up, then starting in the middle of the candle, and 9 strokes going down. Never rub up and then down in the same motion.
- Roll BOTH candles in the POWDER SUGAR.
- Place candles in their candleholders.

Activation
- Light CHARCOAL BLOCK, place in ONE FIREPROOF BOWL and burn INCENSE.
- Meditate on the desired outcome – clear your mind and focus on what you want to accomplish.

Take the RED/PINK THREAD and tie the TWO CANDLES together.

Over the BOWL, melt the bottom of the CANDLES so that they can stand, unaided, in the bowl. Place the CANDLES in the bowl.

As you light the CANDLES recite,

> **From this day forth**
> **May the friendship we hold so dear**
> **Move beyond its current boundaries**
> **Into a love of great worth**
> **With mutual respect and harmony.**

After the candles melt down and the wax is cool, take the wax and place it in the RED CLOTH and tie it closed with the 2nd RED/PINK RIBBON. Place inside your pillow.

If in three months the friendship has not moved in the direction you desire, bury the wax and repeat the spell.

Make Yourself Irresistible To The One You Want

The Best Time
Cast this spell when the moon is new, waxing or full.

The Best Day
Friday

Incense To Use (choose one)
Frankincense, Rosemary, Strengthen a Love #1, Strengthen a Love #2, Boost Your Sex Life #1, Boost Your Sex Life #2

Herbs To Use
Thyme

Oils To Use (choose one)
Date Energy, Lavender

Candles To Use
None

Stones To Use
Amethyst

Other Supplies Needed
Clothes you will wear for next meet, Washing Machine, Laundry Detergent, Distilled Water, One Small Glass, One Large Glass, Plastic Wrap, One Fireproof Bowl (non-metal), One Charcoal Block

Preparation
• Gather supplies

Activation
• Light CHARCOAL BLOCK, place in ONE FIREPROOF BOWL and burn INCENSE.

• Meditate on the desired outcome – clear your mind and focus on what you want to accomplish.

Take your AMETHYST and ask it for its help and guidance. Touch it to the middle of your forehead and to your heart. Kiss it gently.

Place the Amethyst into your projective hand (right if right handed – left if left handed). Visualize your desire to be as irresistible as possible to the one you want. Feel the emotions associated. Once you can no longer hold the image or feel the emotions, then the energy has moved from you into the stone.

Thank the Amethyst for its assistance and place it in the SMALL GLASS.

Fill the LARGE GLASS half way with the DISTILLED WATER. Put the SMALL GLASS into the LARGE GLASS and seal the top with PLASTIC WRAP.

Set out outside or on a windowsill for seventy-two hours (twenty-four hours minimum).

Put YOUR CLOTHES into the WASHING MACHINE. Add the DETERGENT to the manufacturers instructions. When the wash cycle begins, pour the AMETHYST ELIXIR into the water.

During the final rinse cycle, add nine drops of your OIL of choice and three pinches of THYME.

Wear the washed clothes the next time you see the one you want.

Repeat when needed.

Stop The Ending Of A Relationship

The Best Time
Cast this spell when the moon is full.

The Best Day
Friday

Incense To Use (choose one)
Frankincense, Rosemary, Create a Peaceful and Loving Environment

Herbs To Use
Eucalyptus, Rose Petals

Oils To Use (choose one)
Love-Healing-Purification, Lavender

Candles To Use
One Red, Two Blue

Stones To Use
None

Other Supplies Needed
Three Candleholders, Two Fireproof Bowls (non-metal), One Charcoal Block

Preparation
- Gather supplies
- In one BOWL, mix together equal parts of EUCALYPTUS and ROSE PETALS. Put off to the side.
- Carve "Your Name" into the 1st BLUE candle, "Your Partner's Name" into the 2nd BLUE candle and "Love" into the RED candle.

- Place the each candle into your projective hand (right if right handed – left if left handed) to empower it. Visualize your need; feel the emotions associated with it. Once you can no longer hold the image or feel the emotions, then the energy has moved from you into the candle. Empower "You" into the 1st BLUE candle, "Your Partner" into the 2nd BLUE candle and "Reconciliation" into the RED candle.
- Anoint ALL CANDLES with the OIL of choice, using 9 strokes starting in the middle of the candle, going up, then starting in the middle of the candle, and 9 strokes going down. Never rub up and then down in the same motion.
- Roll ALL the candles in the EUCALYPTUS/ ROSE PETALS MIX.
- Place candles in their candleholders.

Activation
- Light CHARCOAL BLOCK, place in ONE FIREPROOF BOWL and burn INCENSE.
- Meditate on the desired outcome – clear your mind and focus on what you want to accomplish.

Take the 1st BLUE candle and place it in the middle of your workspace. As you light it, recite:

This flame is I
My soul, my essence
As it burns
So burns my desire to make all wrongs right.

Take the 2nd BLUE candle. Place it next to the 1st BLUE candle. As you light it, recite:

This flame is (Insert Name)
His/her soul, his/her essence
As it burns
So burns his/her desire to make all wrongs right.

Take the RED candle and place it behind the BLUE candles, so that you form a mini triangle. As you light it, recite:

With the flame
I proclaim
That our love can survive
As we are strong
May our problems be gone.

Mediate on the goal of your love surviving the difficult, reforming and moving forward with him/her in a loving, committed relationship. Once that goal is visualized, the energy work has begun.

Let the candles burn down or for at least nine minutes. If you must extinguish the flame, do so with a snuffer as blowing will scatter the energy. Bury the wax.

Encourage Friendship

The Best Time
Cast this spell when the moon is new, waxing or full.

The Best Day
Friday

Incense To Use (choose one)
Frankincense, Rosemary, Attract Friendship #1, Attract
Friendship #2

Herbs To Use (choose one)
Passion Flower, Sweet Pea, Lemon (zest)

Oils To Use (choose one)
Love and Friendship, Lavender

Candles To Use
Six Pink

Stones To Use (choose one)
Lodestone, Chrysoprase

Other Supplies Needed
Six Candleholders, One Fireproof Bowl (non-metal), One
Charcoal Block

Preparation
- Gather supplies
- Anoint ALL CANDLES with the OIL of choice, using 9 strokes
  starting in the middle of the candle, going up, then starting in
  the middle of the candle, and 9 strokes going down. Never
  rub up and then down in the same motion.
- Roll ALL the candles in the HERB of choice.
- Place candles in their candleholders.

Activation

- Light CHARCOAL BLOCK, place in ONE FIREPROOF BOWL and burn INCENSE.
- Meditate on the desired outcome – clear your mind and focus on what you want to accomplish.

Take the STONE of choice and ask it for its help and guidance. Touch it to the middle of your forehead and to your heart. Kiss it gently.

Place the stone into your projective hand (right if right handed – left if left handed). Visualize the friendship you wish to encourage. Feel the emotions associated with this friendship. Once you can no longer hold the image or feel the emotions, then the energy has moved from you into the stone.

Thank the stone for its help and place it in the middle of your workstation.

Take the PINK candles. Starting at NOON and going clockwise, place the candles the STONE. Light the candles in the order you placed them as you recite:

**In this magical spirit I infuse my wish
My desire and my goal
For a rewarding and mutually satisfying friendship (with Insert
Name if a specific person is desired).**

Visualize on the goal of finding the friendship you want. Once that goal is visualized, the energy work has begun.

Let the candles burn down or for at least nine minutes. If you must extinguish the flame, do so with a snuffer as blowing will scatter the energy. Bury the wax.

Carry the stone with you in your pocket, purse or briefcase until the friendship manifests itself.

Protect Your Relationship From Outside Negativity

The Best Time
Cast this spell when the moon is full.

The Best Day
Sunday or Thursday

Incense To Use (choose one)
Frankincense, Rosemary, Protect Your Space from Unwanted Energy

Herbs To Use
Basil, Cinnamon, Caraway, Salt

Oils To Use (choose one)
Protection, Olive

Candles To Use
Two White, Five Blue

Stones To Use
None

Other Supplies Needed
Seven Candleholders, Two Fireproof Bowls (non-metal), One Charcoal Block

Preparation
- Gather supplies
- In BOWL, mix together equal parts of BASIL, CINNAMON and CARAWAY – set aside.
- Carve "Your Name" into the 1st WHITE candle, "Your Partner's Name" into the 2nd WHITE candle and "Protection" into the BLUE candles.

- Place the each candle into your projective hand (right if right handed – left if left handed) to empower it. Visualize your need; feel the emotions associated with it. Once you can no longer hold the image or feel the emotions, then the energy has moved from you into the candle. Empower "You" into 1st WHITE candle, "Your Partner" into the 2nd WHITE candle and "White Light" into the BLUE candles.
- Anoint ALL CANDLES with the OIL of choice, using 9 strokes starting in the middle of the candle, going up, then starting in the middle of the candle, and 9 strokes going down. Never rub up and then down in the same motion.
- Roll the WHITE the candles in the HERBAL MIXTURE and the BLUE candles in SALT
- Place candles in their candleholders.

Activation

- Light CHARCOAL BLOCK, place in ONE FIREPROOF BOWL and burn INCENSE.
- Meditate on the desired outcome – clear your mind and focus on what you want to accomplish.

Place the two WHITE candles in the center of your work space. As you light them recite:

> **These flames are us**
> **Our souls burn as one**

Put the BLUE candles, starting at NOON, around the WHITE candles in a counterclockwise fashion. As you light them in the order they were placed recite:

> **This wall of protection**
> **Spread the reach of your white light**
> **Far and wide**
> **To keep us safe from those who wish us harm.**

Repel the negativity
And let it disintegrate
Through time and space
So that harm comes to none.

Visualize a white light that surrounds you and your partner, where negativity bounces off its protective boundaries and all that enters your sacred realm is peace, love and harmony. Once you can hold that image in your minds eye, the energy work has begun.

Let the candles burn down or for at least nine minutes. If you must extinguish the flame, do so with a snuffer as blowing will scatter the energy. Bury the wax.

Remove A Love Curse

The Best Time
Cast this spell when the moon is full or waning

The Best Day
Sunday or Thursday

Incense To Use (choose one)
Frankincense, Rosemary, Lift a Curse #1, Lift a Curse #2, Lift a Curse #3

Herbs To Use
Salt, Dried Garlic, Dried Onions, Chili Pepper

Oils To Use (choose one)
Banishment, Eucalyptus

Candles To Use
None

Stones To Use
Nine small stones from a crossroads

Other Supplies Needed
Two Fireproof Bowls (non-metal), Paper, Pen, One Charcoal Block

Preparation
- Gather supplies
- Wash dirt and grime off of STONES
- In BOWL, mix together equal parts of SALT, DRIED GARLIC, DRIED ONIONS, CHILI PEPPER – set aside

Activation
- Light CHARCOAL BLOCK, place in ONE FIREPROOF BOWL and burn INCENSE.
- Meditate on the desired outcome – clear your mind and focus on what you want to accomplish.

Take the STONES and ask them for its help and guidance.
Touch them to the middle of your forehead and to your heart.
Kiss gently.

Place the stones into your projective hand (right if right handed – left
if left handed). Visualize the being lifted and the emotions associated with being free. Once you can no longer hold the image or feel
the emotions, then the energy has moved from you into the stones.

Thank the stones for their help.

Anoint the STONES with the OIL of your choice. Place them
into the BOWL.

*Take the PAPER and PEN and write YOUR name and all other names
associated with being cursed. Next write "CURSE BE GONE" (all in
capital letters). Fold the paper in half, then a fourth, etc…until you get a
small square of paper. Place the square on top of the stones.

Sprinkle the HERBAL MIXTURE on top of the paper. Light the
PAPER so that it and the HERBS burn. As they burn recite:

I announce
My/our misfortune reversed
The curse is returned to the universe
And the black energy dispersed.

Starting at your head, pass a section of your body at a time through
the smoke. As the paper and herbs burn, visualize your misfortune
falling away from you and those associated with the curse.

When the stones and ashes cool off, return all to the
crossroads. Go home without looking back.

*If all who feel that they are involved in the curse could be
present, then this would give the spell an extra burst of energy.
Make sure each person writes his/her name on the paper and
passes his/her body through the smoke.

Notes

Afterward

The best magic one can do involves personal design and self-casting. I hope that the information in this book has stirred your creativity to do just that.

We all have the power within us to manifest change in our lives. Follow your heart, do what feels right and allow your power to determine the success of the magic.

Empower your life and live your dreams!

Recommended Suppliers

The Wiccan Way Online Store

Phone: 469-358-3177
info@wiccanway.com
http://www.wiccanway.com

A bit of everything for all of your magical needs:

- Books
- Videos
- Candles
- Incense
- Herbs
- Oils
- Jewelry
- Kits
- Divination supplies
- Ritual supplies

And so much more!

PsychicHannah.com

Phone: 615-676-9679
thepsychichannah@yahoo.com
http://www.psychichannah.com
http://www.jdvisionsinc.com

See our selection of:

- Blessed Candles
- Oils
- Hoodoo
- Bath/Body
- Ritual Spell Tools
- Crystals
- Herbs
- Accurate Psychic Advice through Tarot, Spirit, Energy Work

And so much more!

Useful Web Links

Dancing Dragonfly
dances@dancing-dragonfly.com
http://www.dancing-dragonfly.com/
(Crystals and stones)

Flower Essence Services
24 hr Order Line: 800-548-0075
Direct Phone Line: 530-265-0258
http://www.fesflowers.com/tfeo1.htm
(Pure essential oils)

The Magickal Cat
questions@themagickalcat.com
24 hr Fax Line: 877-805-1428
http://www.themagickalcat.com/
(Magical supplies in the US)

The Eye of the Cat
eyeofthecat@charter.net
http://www.eyeofthecat.net/
(Magical supplies in the US)

Spellements
info@spellements.com
Phone: 0702 1123332
http://www.spellements.com/
(Magical supplies in the UK)

The Realm of White Magic
whitemagic@whitemagic.com.au
http://www.magic.com.au/
(Magical supplies in Australia)

Burpee
custserv@burpee.com
Customer Service Phone: 800-333-5808
http://www.burpee.com/
(Herb/plant seeds)

Gurney's Seed and Nursery
Customer Service Phone: 513- 354-1492
http://gurneys.com/
(Herb/plant seeds)

Strega Moon Candles
customerservice@stregamooncandles.com
http://www.stregamoon.com/
(Natural candles)

Candle Bee Farm
beekeeper@candlebeefarm.com
http://www.candlebeefarm.com/
(Beeswax candles)

Bibliography

Cunningham, Scott. Cunningham's Encyclopedia of Magical Herbs. St. Paul Minnesota: Llewellyn Publications, 1998.

Cunningham, Scott. Cunningham's Encyclopedia of Crystal, Gem and Metal Magic. St. Paul Minnesota: Llewellyn Publications, 1995.

Cunningham, Scott. Magical Aromatherapy. St. Paul Minnesota: Llewellyn Publications, 1996.

Melody. Love is in the Earth – A Kaleidoscope of Crystals. Wheat Ridge Colorado: Earth-Love Publishing House, 1998

Sharp, Anne Wallace. The Gypsies. San Diego Califorina : Lucent Books, 2003.

The Patrin Web Journal - http://www.geocities.com/Paris/5121/patrin.htm

Empower Your Life

With Personalized Support!

You meditate, you set goals, you read all the new age books -- and your reward? A sea of headaches as things stay the same or, worse yet – become embroiled in chaos!

If you're ready to make a real change, then it's time for an Empowerment Coach, one you can turn to for support, for advice -- one who will make you accountable and help you succeed.

Just think: In as little as one month from today, your mirror can show you a rejeuvinanted, more confident you.

Essential Elements of Empowerment Coaching:

1. Begin by setting a target date to achieve your objectives.

2. Then, you and your coach will set goals that you – yourself – want to achieve.

3. Working together, your coach will help you meet your objectives, step by step.

4. Your coach will help you maximize what you've learned during the process.

5. Your coach will also encourage you and work with you as you learn to take control of the process yourself.

6. Continuous planning and goal-setting will help you refine and meet your objectives.

7. As you learn from the process, your coach will help you identify patterns of behavior – and how to change them.

8. No excuses – your coach will be there to make sure that you work the process completely to make all your dreams come true.

Empowerment Coaching can help you with:

- Discovering your passion

- Making a goal plan

- Finding balance

- Improving magical skills

- Developing meditation techniques

- Connecting with your guides

- Unlocking your psychic abilities

- Understanding dreams

As your own personal Empowerment Coach, Allie can help you identify your goals and then help you focus on achieving them. As a result, you'll find balance and inner harmony while gaining new insight and strength as you empower your life – and live your dreams!

No matter where you are, help is only a phone call and/or email away.

Don't wait – call or visit http://www.GypsyAdvice.com/empowermentcoach.htm or call 330.264.9977 to learn more and set up your own RISK-FREE "Get Acquainted" session!

Empowerment E-Classes

Attempting to work your own magic can be an exercise in hopelessness. Perhaps you get confused on what herbs, oils or candles will work best. Or, your frustration builds when you see little or no results for your efforts.

Don't give up. Together in our Empowerment E-Classes we can help you, whether you're looking to:

• Write and cast your own magic

• Manifest your goals into reality

• Work with and prepare flower essence blends

From the comfort of your own home, you can discover the techniques you need to create your magic, understand it and apply it to your life.

Allie holds e-classes via email with a limit of only 25 participants! Simply turn in assignments via email, discuss, and ask questions as Allie works with you to unlock your own potential…and achieve success.

But you can't do anything unless you act now.

Visit http://www.GypsyAdvice.com/empowermenteclasses.htm or call 330.264.9977 for more information and to secure your spot.

Empowerment Workshops

Striving to connect to the Divine can be an exercise in frustration. Perhaps you get discouraged when you can't seem to connect. Or, you can't focus your energies enough to make any sort of connection possible.

Don't give up. Together in our Empowerment Workshops we can help you, whether you're looking to:

• Maximize your psychic abilities

• Contact and work with your guides and angels

• Discover past lives

• Find your soul mate

• Decode your dreams

From the comfort of your own home, you can discover the techniques you need to make that connection, understand it and apply it to your life.

Allie holds workshops via teleconference with a limit of only 25 participants! Simply call in using your own phone and listen, discuss, and ask questions as Allie works with you to unlock your own potential...and achieve success.

But you can't do anything unless you act now.

Visit http://www.GypsyAdvice.com/empowermentworkshops.htm or call 330.264.9977 for more information and to secure your spot.

Prefer to attend a workshop in person? Visit http://www. GypsyAdvice.com/empowermentworkshops.htm to discover when Allie will be in a town near you!

About the Author

Allie is an internationally renowned Personal Intuitive Advisor with a thriving practice in Ohio. A descendant of the Rom gypsies of Transylvania, she is blessed with the gifts of clairvoyance (seeing psychic visions), claircognizance (knowing facts without knowing how one receives the information), clairaudience (hearing the voice of the Divine), energy/light healing, prophecy and the knack with communicating with her spirit guides and angels.

She lives in the heart of Ohio's Amish country with her family and pets.

Her syndicated metaphysical advice column, *Ask Allie*, is available on over fifty web sites and her Podcast is heard around the world.

To schedule book signing, please visit Gypsy Girl Press at http://www.GypsyGirlPress.net for more information.

To schedule a reading or workshop, please visit Allie's web site, Gypsy Advice, at http://www.GypsyAdvice.com

Made in the USA
Charleston, SC
23 September 2011